Intermediate
Level

SIERRA NEVADA SUITE

6 ORIGINAL PIANO SOLOS

By John S. Hord

ISBN 978-1-5400-4682-6

EXCLUSIVELY DISTRIBUTED BY

HAL•LEONARD®

Visit Hal Leonard Online at
www.halleonard.com

Contact us:
Hal Leonard
7777 West Bluemound Road
Milwaukee, WI 53213
Email: info@halleonard.com

In Europe, contact:
Hal Leonard Europe Limited
42 Wigmore Street
Marylebone, London, W1U 2RN
Email: info@halleonardeurope.com

In Australia, contact:
Hal Leonard Australia Pty. Ltd.
4 Lentara Court
Cheltenham, Victoria, 3192 Australia
Email: info@halleonard.com.au

Performance Notes

This suite is an homage to dance and music forms of the Baroque era coupled with a deep love of the beauty of the Sierra Nevada in California. The Sierra Nevada is a mountain range that extends north to south in eastern California. Its length is 440 miles; California is 770 miles in length.

Crystal Cave (Basso Ostinato)

Since a cave is below ground, I thought it appropriate to compose a ground bass. The ground was a prominent music form in the Baroque. The ground is a short melodic phrase repeated continually and usually in, but not restricted to, the bass. The ground bass is in the left hand, measures 1 through 3. I used a descending chromatic line to emulate water slowly running down the sides of a cave. Crystal Cave is enormous. It has high ceilings allowing many unusual sounds and easy viewing. Imagine strolling through this cave while taking in the beautiful sights and sounds. One room of the cave is named the Organ Room. Dozens of stalactites and stalagmites look like pipes of a pipe organ. This is illustrated in measures 21 through 24. The final measure is the flurry of bats that take flight from the cave each evening.

Mount Whitney (Bourdon)

Bourdon is defined as a low note of long duration; e.g., drone or pedal point (pipe organ). In 17th century France society it was exemplified by the Musette and hurdy-gurdy. In measures 1–6 the right-hand music imitates the slow ascent of the mountain and the inevitable two-steps-forward-one-step-back procedure. Measure 9 begins the descent and ends in jubilation of conquering the mountain. The piece ends with a plagal (Amen) cadence. I thought this fitting as a thankful end to the arduous journey over Mount Whitney, giving thanks for the natural beauty and life of the Sierra Nevada.

Pesky Pests (Bourrée)

The bourrée originated as a peasant dance in France during the 17th century. It is a dance in quick duple time beginning with an upbeat. It is to be light and full of the joy of life. This humorous bourrée depicts insects buzzing around our faces and imitates the frantic gestures made by people trying to control the tiny critters. The piece ends triumphantly with the left hand ascending through G harmonic minor into G Major and then the hand slap.

Rafting on the Kings River (Toccata)

The Kings River winds its way through Kings Canyon National Park down to the San Joaquin Valley, dropping in elevation from 14,000 feet to 200 feet. The river is fast and wild in spring and early summer as the snowmelt races down to the valley. Once a raft sets off on the river it is a wild ride, much like performing a toccata. Imagine yourself and others in a large rubber raft hurling down the river at great speeds, the icy cold water splashing your face and the roar of the water so loud you can hear nothing else. And, sometimes there are unexpected crashes, illustrated at the end of this piece.

Redwoods (Prelude)

Many of the preludes composed for keyboard in the Baroque era were based on chord progressions. *Redwoods* begins with a chord progression in a figuration similar to the C Major Prelude from J.S. Bach's *Well-Tempered Clavier, Book I*. The chord progression is ascending to represent one's gaze traveling up the tall redwoods.

The melody at measures 19 through 21 is *Ubi Caritas*, plainsong, Mode 6. I have included this portion of the plainsong to highlight the sense of sanctuary that is present in a grove of redwoods. It should be played with rhythmic freedom, the plainsong singing through your fingers. The redwoods of the Sierra Nevada average age is 2,000 to 3,000 years; typical height is 250 to 300 feet; average diameter is 28 to 32 feet. Redwoods prefer to grow in groves.

Snow Plant (Da Capo Aria)

An aria is a composition for solo voice with instrumental accompaniment. The term "aria" was also used for a short instrumental piece with a song-like quality and was often used as a single movement in a suite. The *Da Capo Aria* was the favored aria form in the Baroque era. The new aspect of this aria form was the introduction of repeating the A section creating the A-B-A structure so common in music and nature. The snow plant pops out of the ground during snowmelt in spring. It is bright red. It has no chlorophyll and lives on fungi found below ground. It prefers to grow in colonies. In *Snow Plant*, the contrasting sounds of the A and B sections are to emulate two contrasting moods. The pleasant beauty of E-flat major illustrates the beauty of the forest in spring when all is fresh. The B section illustrates the plaintive loneliness of being the first flower to bloom. Let the aria sing like a crystalline mountain breeze through pine boughs.

CONTENTS

Crystal Cave
Basso ostinato (Ground bass)

By John S. Hord

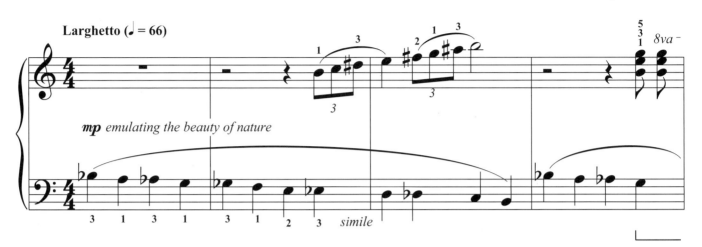

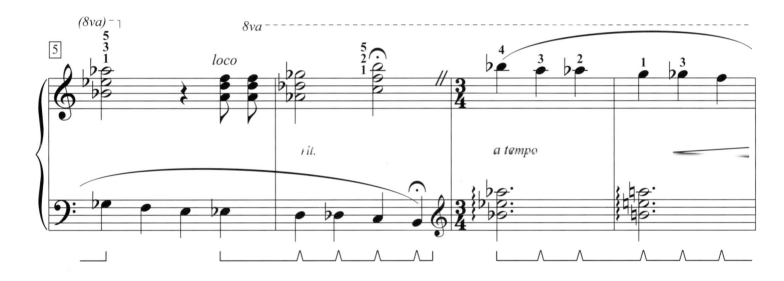

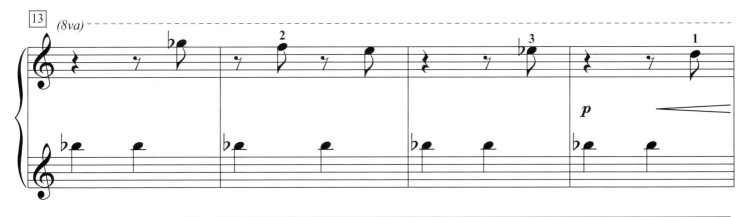

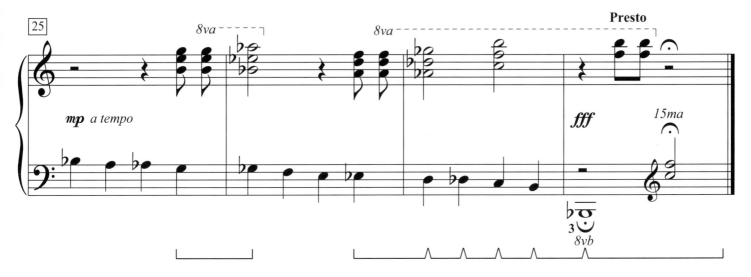

Pesky Pests
Bourrée

By John S. Hord

Allegro (♩ = 132)

L.H. staccato throughout

Use L.H. to slap the
top of your R.H. wrist.

Rafting on the Kings River

Toccata

By John S. Hord

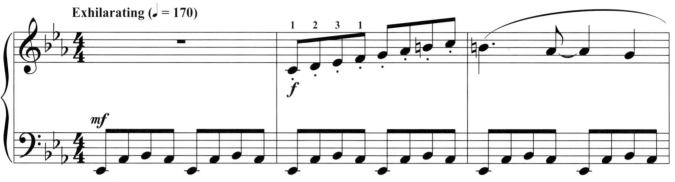

Performer may use legato or staccato touch in the L.H.

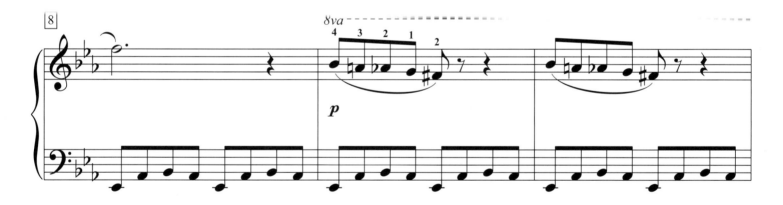

9

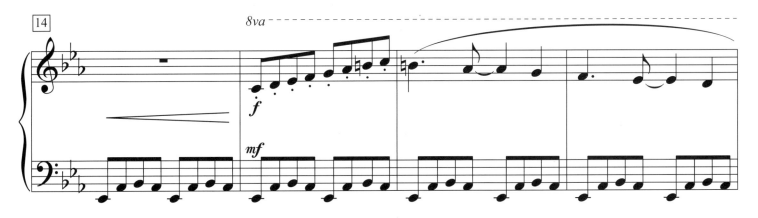

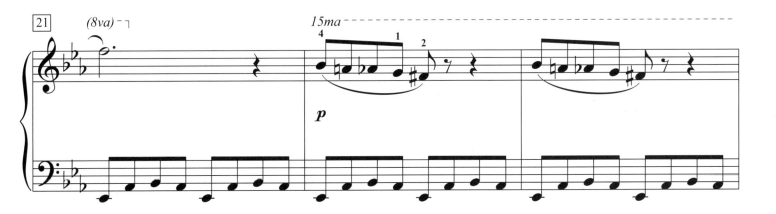

Mount Whitney
Bourdon

By John S. Hord

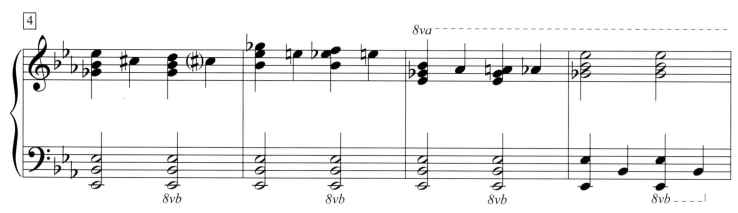

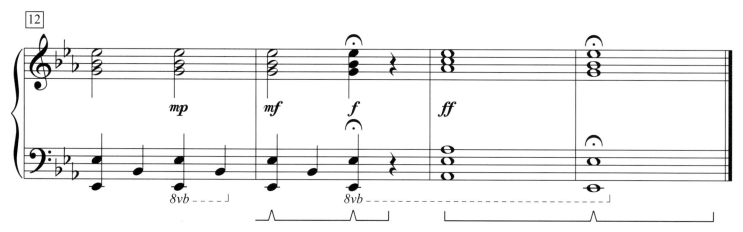

Redwoods
Prelude

By John S. Hord

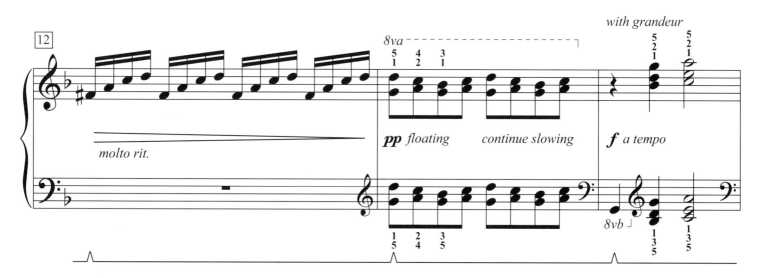

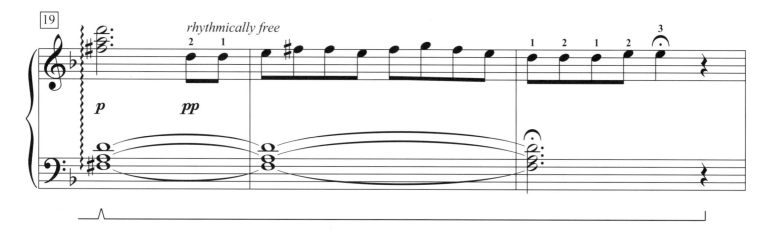

for my wife, Margaret

Snow Plant
Da Capo Aria

By John S. Hord

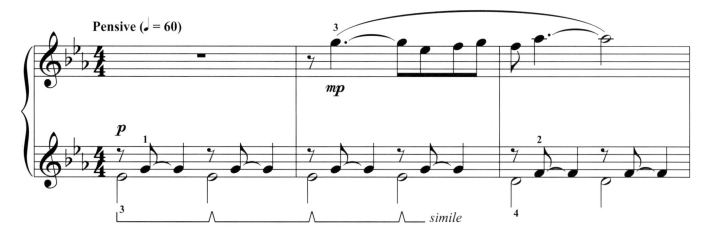
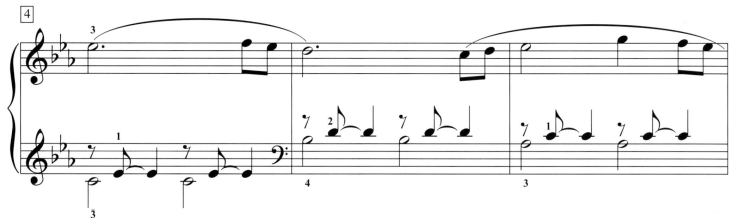
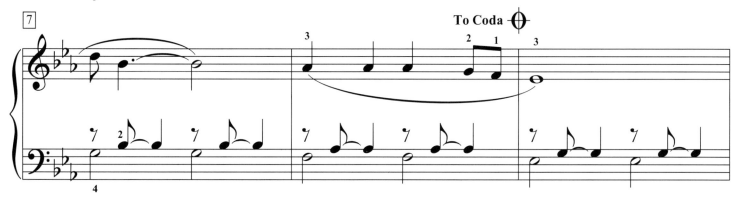

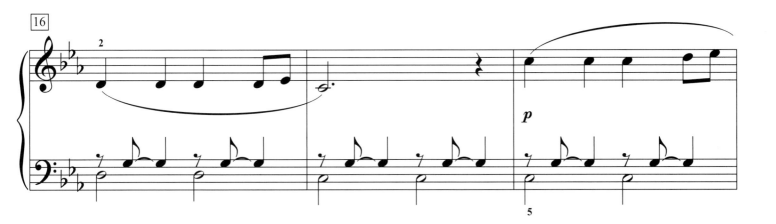

16

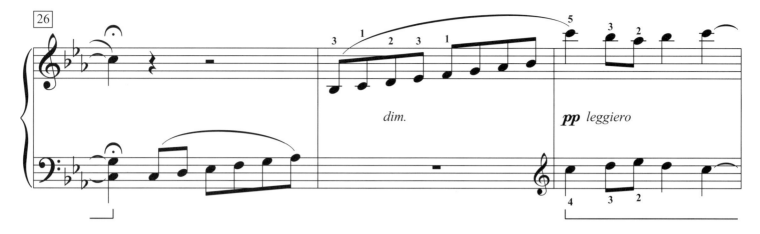

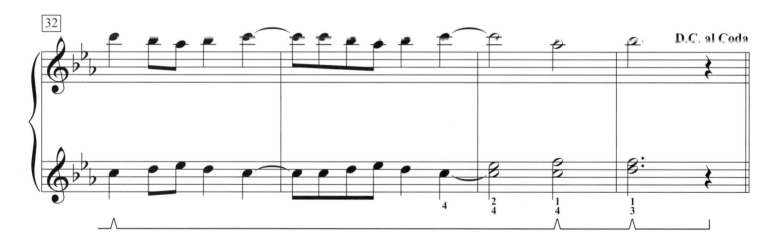